Connecting: Key Networking Tips For Business And Life

103 proven strategies to increase business and build relationships

by William M. Saleebey, Ph.D.

Connecting: Key Networking Tips For Business And Life

Copyright © 2016 by William M. Saleebey, Ph.D.

Cover by: Kurt Michelson

ISBN-13: 978-1523833825
ISBN-10: 1523833823

www.DrBillSaleebey.com
Email: wsaleeb@gmail.com

Printed in U.S.A.

Forward by Keith Ferrazzi

TABLE OF CONTENTS

William M. Saleebey, Ph.D.

This book is gratefully dedicated to the late Dr. Louis F. Markert, my friend since 1974 graduate school at UCLA. Lou was always encouraging and supportive. He was a great listener, and he is greatly missed. Whenever I had a project, he applauded me with superlatives. Lou and I walked hundreds of miles and talked about everything. He greatly enriched my life and is an inspiration to me and a continued guide to my thinking.

Acknowledgments

There are many people who helped inspire me to write this book, and who contributed significantly to the process. Eddie Neiman was a huge inspiration, and acted as a coach to make sure I was accountable to my goals. This is a true networking story. I first met Eddie when he did the loan for my first home purchase, got to know him through Bruin Professionals and then ProVisors, we worked on Chapter Development together, and then became friends in the process.

Joe Wingard, current President of Bruin Professionals is a true mentor, huge booster of my business, and another person who became a friend through the networking process. Other key Bruin Professionals influencers in the process have been Randy Sheinbein, Scott Redston, Todd Moster, Barbara Schwartz, Katherine Dickerson and Andy Jacobs.

I want to give thanks to all those who read drafts of the book and provided useful feedback. Deb Rodney, Jim Picker, Marv Kaye, Keith Gregory and Peter Finkel all assisted in shaping the final product. Kurt Michelson did a brilliantly creative job on the cover design. C. Spencer Reynolds was indispensable in handling the layout, design and publishing of the book and audiobook.

Special thanks to the late Gordon Gregory for a huge assistance in getting my name on the networking map, my LA3 and ProVisors family far and wide, and the many people who have encouraged my work.

To my friends and family for always reminding me to believe in myself. To my late cousins Beez and Linda, who really knew what networking was all about. I am grateful for my children, grandchildren, nephews and nieces. To Judy, who in her understated way reminds me to believe in myself and that is okay to keep working. She also shows every day how networking can be a way of life and enriches our lives.

ABOUT THE AUTHOR

Dr. Bill Saleebey is the foremost expert on the psychological and practical aspects of business networking. He is the author of the books "Connecting: Beyond the Name Tag", "Sell Yourself", and "Study Skills for Success." He has been speaking, training and teaching on a wide variety of topics since 1973. Dr. Saleebey received his Ph.D. in Education with a specialization in Counseling from UCLA. He serves as a consultant and trainer with businesses to infuse networking into their business development practices.

Dr. Saleebey's diverse career has included research on the educational problems of Samoan migrants based on his work on the island of American Samoa which was the basis of his doctoral dissertation, the creation and development of the Study Skills Seminar, and over thirty-three years of business development experience as a relocation manager, currently with American Relocation & Logistics. He facilitates networking groups with ProVisors and Bruin Professionals. He is currently Executive Vice President/President Elect of Bruin Professionals.

Currently, Dr. Saleebey is a keynote speaker, networking coach, business development trainer for corporations, and teaches group leaders how to facilitate the group process. He works with professional firms, educational institutions and a wide variety of businesses to implement effective networking skills into business. His work also includes forming and nurturing the growth of networking groups in industry and with alumni organizations.

If you would like more information about networking skills training, coaching, business development training or speaking, you can connect directly with Dr. Saleebey at wsaleeb@gmail.com or thorough his web site at drbillsaleebey.com.

ENDORSEMENTS

"Having an educator's background, Dr. Saleebey has structured his book with sound pedagogical principles of chunking information, providing illustrative examples, reviewing key concepts. It's a great field manual for the busy professional because it is carved up in bite-sized pieces–easy to digest when I've got a little down-time in-between other work activities. As someone myself who can be intimidated by the length of a book, I'd suggest thinking of Bill's new book as a series of filecards neatly bound in a cover. And, he delivers more than he promises. I like the format being a list of specific tips punctuated with engaging and memorable, then bookended afterward by a series of practical exercises.

As a professional networker, the author understands the importance of maintaining persistence in the networking domain. While persistence and momentum are essential to the networking endeavor, these unfortunately can seem like hard work. As a professional educator and therapist, he emphasizes a concept of "netplaying," that I like a lot. It is much easier to maintain persistence and build momentum if you are doing things you enjoy and would do anyway because your are just having fun."

James J. De Santis, Ph.D.
Clinical Psychologist
Author, The Business of Practice

"I want everyone to read it. Bill's book is empowering – he shares the secrets and makes it easy to learn—and practice—networking skills he spent years perfecting. Follow these tips to develop your own power networks and friendships. It's an extra bonus to have topics and exercises for improving our networking skills and leading groups!"

Penny Peak, Alumni Director

"This book is an absolute gem. It covers every conceivable aspect of how to be successful in networking for both business and life in general. Saleebey's understanding of the networking process from both a personal and business perspective is very impressive, and his ability to simplify concepts and make them accessible to every reader are plainly evident from page one. The networking tips are very easy to understand and apply, and will benefit both beginners and seasoned professionals alike. This is a must-read for anyone who works with other people, for compensation or as a volunteer, in the private or public sector. I highly recommend it for personal use and in networking groups as a training vehicle."

Joseph A. Wingard, MBA, Ph.D.
President, Bruin Professionals

"Bill's latest book about networking is not only for someone just trying to learn how to network. This book provides valuable lessons for even the most experienced networker. We all have something to learn and Bill is a terrific teacher and mentor."

Keith Gregory, Partner
Snell & Wilmer

"I invite you to explore the pages of Dr Bill Saleebey's book. Bill covers everything you need to know about professional networking and how to maximize the experience. This book is a clear, easy to use guide for creating impactful connections and getting the most value from these priceless relationships.

Nikki Potter, CEO
ProVisors

"A MUST READ for anyone looking to be an effective networking professional! There is something in this book for everyone! Whether you are just getting started or you have been networking for 30 years – invest in yourself and your business and read Connecting! One area we just don't spend enough time is how to effectively make strong and valuable connections. Bill has compiled treasure trove of insights to help you deliver fantastic results! Read Connecting today!"

Michael D. Preston
BTI Certified Business Coach / Speaker / Trainer

"The challenge of conducting business in 21st Century America can appear overwhelming. Competition is more cutthroat than ever. Technology, social conventions and effective business models seem to change by the hour. Social media and other forms of communication present a dizzying and almost paralyzing number of outreach choices.

Fortunately, business networking expert Bill Saleebey, author of "Connecting: Beyond the Name Tag", "Sell Yourself" and "Study Skills for Success," is back to save the day. In fact, his new book, "Connecting: Key Networking Tips for Business and Life," is like a warm, comforting glass of milk on a blustery evening.

Combining common sense, ethics and time-tested networking techniques with real-time examples and amusing anecdotes, Dr. Saleebey brings us back to a core notion that is as likely to be relevant in 2116 as it is in 2016. Successful businesses, he convincingly argues, are based upon trusted and effective communication between caring human beings. To that end, he provides a series of concise tips and exercises designed to catapult the most complacent, staid businessperson into action and profitability.

It doesn't hurt that Dr. Saleebey serves up his recipe of enduring truths and surefire strategies in an amusing, crisply-written narrative. Whether you're a business leader, entrepreneur, salesperson, politician or social worker, "Connecting" will provide the tools you need for professional success.

Todd Moster, Esq.
Director, Recruitment & Placement
Moster Legal Placement, Inc.

Dr. Saleebey is the foremost expert on networking. This book breaks many aspects of networking down into bite size nuggets that can be easily understood, learned, practiced, perfected and executed. Anyone who prospects and sells everyday for his livelihood should have in their toolbox. I highly endorse Dr. Bill and his latest book.

Eddie Neiman
Certified Mortgage Planning Specialist

Dr. Bill Saleebey's book provides outstanding pearls of networking wisdom which are concise and easy to read. He shows how networking goes beyond business to become a way of life for anyone, regardless of background or personality. Bill fully understands the networking process and shows us how to make it work in all situations by being giving, genuine, and ethical.

Deborah Rodney, Regional Director
ProVisors

This book by Dr. Bill Saleebey is full of very practical steps that every professional or small business owner can use to become a great networker.

It is a must-read for both the novice and seasoned pro who is really serious about building his or her business.

Marv Kaye, J.D., CFP®
Kaye Capital Management

FORWARD

As long as I can remember, I've been keenly aware of the importance of developing strong, supportive relationships. We may like to think of ourselves as rugged individualists, but the truth is no one has achieved any level of success on his or her own. We're hardwired to be tribal. We need other people in all facets of our lives.

Relationships, and the art and science of building them, have long been a focus in my career, first in the business world at Deloitte and Starwood Hotels and later as a writer, thought leader and entrepreneur. It's the foundation of my current work, as CEO of Ferrazzi Greenlight and of onboarding platform Yoi, and has become second nature to many of us.

While people across industries and cultures are being urged to network, whether by their managers, friends, family or the articles they read each day, they often don't have a clue how to get started. Networking shouldn't be just another sales pitch but a process where adding value and giving to others are central elements. You have to know and trust each other before you can be of service to one another, but finding a way to connect with another person quickly and deeply can be daunting.

With Connecting: Key Networking Tips for Business and Life, William M. Saleebey finds the right balance of psychology and business to lessen that intimidation since he was his very first "test case" teaching himself how to overcome these obstacles and becoming a true thought leader on the subject.

By combining tips, exercises and personal stories, Saleebey breaks the process down into easily understood and enacted practices that make it crystal clear and very user-friendly for his audience. Readers are urged to look at themselves candidly and apply the principles immediately, and repeatedly, in all aspects of their lives to create lasting behavior change.

This book clearly represents the new wave of networking that encourages people to embrace technology as a tool to build mutually beneficial personal and business relationships and to present themselves in an authentic manner to become more successful.

-Keith Ferrazzi, author of "Never Eat Alone"

INTRODUCTION

This is a book about networking. It addresses business development through networking, and the building of personal networks that can aid in a myriad of endeavors such as business development, job search, inbound and outbound referrals, gaining and giving strategic introductions, and simply having a viable network. Because of the rapidly increasing and changing presence of social media, some concepts will be outdated sooner than others. Most of the psychological principles will remain intact for many years. The primary analysis and research that led to this book took place in metropolitan areas of the western United States. Some of the tips and culturally-related concepts would certainly vary in other regions and countries.

This book is a companion to Connecting: Beyond the Name Tag (2009). Beyond the Name Tag was more of an introduction that focussed on an analysis of where business meets psychology. Connecting: Key Networking Tips for Business and Life emphasizes specific networking tips and stories that people need to be successful in the networking process. The tips are numerous and cover every conceivable angle of networking. If you understand and practice the tips, you will gain a substantial amount from networking. The networking exercises are intended to be used in networking group meetings to strengthen and deepen relationships

Much has happened since Connecting: Beyond the Name Tag was written and published. Social media has grown in many different ways, and continues to change almost daily. Networking groups have proliferated, and continue to do so. People from many sectors are urging others about the value, I daresay necessity of possessing and utilizing networking strategies, tactics and skills. Some things have stayed virtually constant.

The psychological and sociological principles have not changed much, with the notable exception of the coming of age of millennials, and the resulting burgeoning of all aspects of social media. As the millennials have come of age, the baby boomer generation has become somewhat polarized vis a vis technology and social media.   As a baby boomer, I have noticed that members of my generation vary widely in their use and embracing technology and social media. People who are still actively in business, specifically business development, tend to embrace the basics of technology such as texting, LinkedIn and Facebook.

Personally, I ditched my AOL e-mail account in favor of Gmail due to Gmail's superior service and reputation.   Thus, the generation that has grown up on social media and technology, especially smart phones and texting, have never known devices such as pagers and totally eschew things like land lines, handwritten letters and AOL. Some are reluctant to use the phone because they feel that it is an intrusion on others.

In terms of networking groups, the elevator speech has become more of a staple, and there have become accepted guidelines for giving a testimonial at a networking meeting. One-sheets, where people can state who they are and what they do on a single sheet they hand out at meetings, have severely decreased due to ecological and paper conservation concerns, at least in California where most of my networking experience has been.

 In my own evolution over the past six years, certain concepts have come into sharper focus and become central to my practice. Personal/business conversations, wide or deep networks, in person versus social media, the concepts of giving and getting involved, and the necessity of building relationships over time have become the MAIN POINTS. They were part of Connecting: Beyond the Name Tag but have stood out as central to the networking process.

The fundamental difference between Connecting: Key Networking Tips for Business and Life and Connecting: Beyond the Name Tag is that this book is much more specifically about Networking Tips, Stories and Exercises, and that is the focus. This book can be used immediately by people who ask the question, "What do I need to do to become successful in networking" or "How do I build, nurture and sustain my network?" Networking is more about building relationships for business and career development. Once you have built that network, nurtured and fed it, it is yours for the rest of your life, and no one can take it away from you. It is golden because success is as much about who you know as what you know.

WHO SHOULD READ THIS BOOK

This book is specifically designed for busy professionals who want to gain maximal and ever increasing success in business development by applying some proven principles. It is also quite useful for people who will be in search of work or simply want to build a strong, vibrant and beneficial network. Anyone can read this book, because the principles extend beyond business development and are based on proven psychological principles and ethical values. It is designed for both beginning and experienced networkers. For sustainable results, networking should be a way of life.

WHAT IS THIS BOOK

It is a kind of tool kit of many simple and immediately useful tips, guides, strategies and tactics that have been used by thousands of people in a wide variety of careers and professional settings. Many have been gleaned from high level networking groups, and others from life. It is the author's intention that these tips can be immediately and continually applied. The stories are designed to make the ideas understandable and relevant. Read the tips, stories and exercises in any order you choose.

WHEN SHOULD YOU READ THIS BOOK

There is no time like the present to learn and begin applying this information. You don't need to master it all, or even do it all to derive a significant benefit. You can read one or a few networking tips at a time and try to apply them at your next opportunity. Effective networking is much more about being yourself, real and genuine, and building relationships consistently over time. It is not a quick fix or a way to find a job in a hurry.

REPETITION OF CERTAIN IDEAS AND CONCEPTS IS INTENTIONAL

The most important ideas are intentionally REPEATED for your use and retention. So you may see Tips that look similar, but there are subtle differences to reflect slightly different situations or principles. Besides, repetition is the Mother of Learning.

KEEP AN OPEN MIND

Begin with an open mind and the willingness to try some new things. Your preconception of networking might be different from reality.

WHAT IS NETWORKING

Networking is a process that primarily involves building mutually beneficial relationships with the goal of helping others. It begins with an attitude of giving rather than receiving. If you focus on all of the ways you can help others, such as making referrals, making strategic introductions and putting people together, you will receive bountiful rewards. You can also think about GETTING INVOLVED and raising your hand to volunteer in groups. That is not only the right thing to do, but will raise your profile in the group. That is a good thing in networking. So this book takes a position about the primary importance of giving, building relationships over time, and being genuine. Networking isn't simply smiling, shaking a lot of hands, collecting (and giving) business cards and working a room. It is much more than that.

ASSUMPTIONS OF READERS

This book is NOT for everyone. The following assumptions will guide you about whether to read the book or not. Of course, if you are a family member, friend or supporter of me and my ideas, read on.

1. You want others to know who you are and what you do for work.

2. You want to know others.

3. You want to increase your business.

4. You want to increase outbound sources for you to refer business and an asset to people in your network.

5. You want to build a quality and vibrant network.

6. You are open-minded.

7. You are willing to go to some networking meetings, other meetings and social events.

8. You are willing to use some forms of social media.

9. You are willing to be yourself.

10. You are willing to be an attentive and interested listener.

11. You are willing to learn how to better express yourself.

12. You are willing to follow up.

13. You will do what you say you are going to do when you say you are going to do it.

14. You are willing to change your opinions of others.

15. You are willing to try and practice new behaviors.

HOW TO BEST USE THESE NETWORKING TIPS

Some of these tips are really serious and business-like. Others are intended to bring a smile to your face or make you laugh. Hopefully you will be able to tell the difference. Think about them, observe them, practice them, talk about them with others. Use the extra space on the pages of this book to take notes on how you plan to use the tips. Have fun with this, then it can really be NETPLAYING and not like work at all. So here we go on this brief but very important journey...

TIP #1 - GIVE TO OTHERS. LEARN ABOUT THEM AND TRY TO FIND WAYS TO PROVIDE USEFUL INFORMATION AND TRUSTED ADVICE.

Many people join networking groups primarily to increase their business and bank account. I did. What I learned over time was that a more productive attitude was one of GIVING. In order to do that, you need to be an excellent listener and pay attention to what others say and what they need.

As you build your network, your ability to help others increases exponentially. Be willing to share information and make referrals. It is really the attitude of giving that is important. The giving should be done without the expectation of receiving anything in return. But don't worry, if you give, give generously and competently, you will receive abundantly in return.

The networking stories that follow some of the tips are all designed to illustrate certain points. You never know how your responses to situations can impact your success in networking. Enjoy them and learn from them. Perhaps you have some good networking stories of your own.

STORY - TAKING YOUR TIME TO GIVE ADVICE

Several years ago a commercial real estate broker called me to ask me some questions about my commercial relocation business that she needed answered for her client. I didn't know her, but took about twenty minutes answering all of her questions and taking time to assist her, without any expectation of a benefit to me. Coincidentally, I saw her at a networking event the following day. She thanked me privately and in front of the group. That was the beginning of a long and extremely productive mutual relationship. She has given me many enthusiastic referrals to her clients, and introduced me to her associates who also refer me. None of this would have happened if I hadn't taken the time to answer her questions with no expectation of getting anything in return for doing so.

TIP #2 - BE LIKABLE AND PEOPLE ARE MUCH MORE LIKELY TO MAKE REFERRALS AND INTRODUCTIONS TO YOU.

There is a paradigm for networking that really simplifies and explains the process:

KNOW — LIKE — TRUST — REFER/INTRODUCE/ASSIST

The process begins with knowing others and what they do. It's not what you know that is the most important thing, but who you know and who knows you and what you do. So the first step in the networking process is KNOW.

The second step is LIKE. If we don't like someone, it is unlikely that we will be inclined to help them. People are likable for several reasons:

- they are good listeners
- they have positive attitudes
- they smile
- they call you by name
- they remember what you tell them
- they are fun to be around
- they are cheerful
- they are interesting

The networking process is likely to stall or stop if you are not likable. Though it is difficult to actually teach someone to be likable, if you adhere to the principles in the bullets above, you will go a long way toward becoming likable.

The third step is TRUST, and trust is earned by your reputation. Trust is a key step, for you can know and like someone, but if you don't trust them, it is unlikely that you will make referrals, introductions or provide advice to them. The time it takes to truly earn trust varies from situation to situation, and the complexity of the assignment. Trust really refers to the quality of your work, your responsiveness, and how easy it is to work with you.

Likability is so essential to the networking process that it can literally make or break your success in networking. Though it cannot be taught in the same way as other skills like playing the piano, you can learn skills and techniques that will make you increasingly likable. This concept is SO important that it will be intentionally repeated for your retention.

TIP #3 - BASICS OF A POWERFUL ELEVATOR SPEECH/ SELF-INTRODUCTION

Most networking groups, and many other groups, allow people to introduce themselves. The term "elevator speech" came about from the idea that if you are on an elevator on the 14th floor and someone asks you what you do, you could tell them before you hit the ground floor.

The introduction might be your only opportunity in a meeting to describe who you are, your company, and exactly what you do.

Here are some basic principles of the elevator speech:

- Be concise (less is more) - VERY IMPORTANT!!
- Be clear
- Be compelling
- Be memorable
- Have a Call to Action - "Call me when…."
- Speak loudly enough to be heard
- Tell a brief story if you have more time
- Describe your ideal customer
- Clarify the unique value your bring to your clients/customers
- Don't use acronyms or trade jargon
- Don't use cliches
- Use concrete examples to illustrate your points
- Use visual aids/props if appropriate to illustrate what you do

You don't have to do all of the above bulleted items, but be aware of all of them, and use as many as possible for maximal success.

It is a personal choice about whether to write a speech, memorize it and use it every time or vary it from meeting to meeting. Use humor if you are good at it, or work at it if you are not. And don't laugh at your own jokes if you are trying to tickle some funny bones.

TIP #4 - WHERE TO WEAR YOUR NAME TAG

On your right side about shoulder high so when you shake hands the other person can see it. When making name tags, be sure that they are large enough to be easily readable.

TIP #5 - HOW MUCH TO TALK AND HOW MUCH TO LISTEN

It is VERY important to be a GOOD LISTENER. That process starts from being genuinely interested in and curious about the other person, paying attention, and remembering much of what they say. You need to be ready and prepared to talk, but never to dominate and control a conversation.

Here are some tips to be better at conversation:

- Ask open-ended questions that allow the other person to respond
- Clarify if you are unsure of what someone meant
- Stay focused
- Use people's name and what they said in the conversation
- Pay attention to time when talking
- Repeat what others say to aid in retention

Clue: Two ears, one mouth, meant to be used in that proportion.

TIP #6 - SHOW UP CONSISTENTLY AND GET INVOLVED

There is no substitute for SHOWING UP. Not only do you need to attend meetings and events on a regular basis and on time, but you also need to GET INVOLVED. When volunteers are solicited, and you have the time and requisite skills, raise your hand. When you do volunteer to join or lead a committee, always do what you say you are going to do when you say you are going to do it. Your competent involvement is a kind of work sample, and will lead to positive relationships and likely referrals. The opposite is also true. If you are a slacker or flaker, it is unlikely that people will make referrals, introductions or buy from you. How you show up to a meeting, event or troika will be how others will assume you'd show up to a client they refer to you.

The other benefit of getting involved is that you are able to build stronger relationships within the committee, and make it easier to attend the larger events because you know more people. You are building your core group. Getting involved will raise you profile, which is a good thing in a networking or social group.

Get involved and do the best possible job you can do. Do what you promise to do in a timely manner. Be a team player. The more involved you are, the quicker you can become the nexus (center) of the group. Your involvement is a work sample by which others will judge you (hopefully in a very positive light). Only volunteer if you have the time and commitment to follow through. Work with others in a collaborative spirit rather than trying to do everything yourself. Don't boast about the work you have done. Leave that to others, and if you are complimented or singled out for doing a good job, show gratitude gracefully.

STORY - UBIQUITOUS EDDIE

Eddie is a member of two of my networking groups. He is everywhere, going to more meetings than anyone else. By doing so, and getting involved, he has raised his profile quite high in both groups. Another benefit is that because he meets and knows so many people (and is a natural connector) he is able to make and receive many referrals and introductions. He is constantly trying to help others, and in the process has a steady flow of business. His high level of attendance and involvement has made him a center (nexus) of the groups, and go-to person for many situations. The business and personal benefits to Eddie have been profound and widespread. He attributes much of his success to the volume of his networking activity. Additionally, he has formed numerous friendships through this process.

TIP #7 - CONNECT PEOPLE YOU KNOW WITH ONE ANOTHER

Be a connector. One great way to be successful in networking is to put people together who are likely to have some synergy between them. The more people you meet (and learn and remember what they do), the better you will be able to make introductions among them. Be proactive in this process, rather than waiting to be asked to make an introduction.

You can make a personal introduction at a networking meeting or social event, or you can do it electronically. People will appreciate your efforts, and some benefits to you are a likely outcome. However, make introductions (or referrals for that matter) without the expectation of receiving anything in return in the spirit of helping others.

An indirect referral which is an introduction to someone who can make direct referrals is a very useful way to connect people who might have potential value for one another. Both indirect referrals and direct client referrals are quite useful.

One of the most basic and important networking skills is to be a connector. As you learn about people, their business and who they need to know, make introductions. This is best accomplished by first finding out if the introduction is desired, then sending an e-mail of introduction with both people copied. Connect people any chance you get, and this will not only feel good, but will make you a more valuable networking partner.

TIP #8 - BUILD YOUR NETWORK WIDE AND DEEP

How wide or deep you build your network depends on a number of factors. The primary determinants are available time and the nature of your specialization. If you have limited time for business development (like networking) and a fairly common profession, then you might want to be in fewer groups and really get to know everyone in your group (DEEP).

If you have more time and the inclination to network more, then you can attend more diverse groups in a wider geographic area. Regardless of your specialty and available time, you should always be fully present and engaged with whoever you are talking to, and not in a hurry to "mingle". Social media allows you to build a much wider network than in person networking. However, it is best to use both, and use them consistently.

If your business or specialty is unique within a group and your geographic reach is large, you should build a wider network. If your business is common and/or your geographic reach is narrow, then you should go deeper with fewer people.

TIP #9 - HAVE PERSONAL CONVERSATIONS TO BUILD RELATIONSHIPS

In order to build meaningful, productive and long lasting relationships, you need to learn personal things about others and engage in personal as well as business conversations. Many networking conversations start with "What do you do?" That is a normal and essential part of business networking, but in order to really deepen relationships, it is useful to ask "What do you do for fun?" or "Tell me about your hobby" or "Where did you grow up?"

Build on prior conversations by asking pertinent questions about things that have been discussed. If you pay attention, listen intently and remember what has been said, you can progress in the relationship over a long period of time. Though you might have joined a networking group to increase commerce, the camaraderie can lead to friendship. The deeper relationship can then lead to a real sense of community that you develop over time. Without personal conversations you will be limited in the level and depth of relationships. By building strong rapport with others, you can then develop mutually beneficial business and personal relationships.

TIP #10 - SHOW RESPECT TO EVERYONE

Don't be an elitist. Always show respect to everyone. Just because someone is younger, less experienced or less financially successful, you should still show them respect. You should do this because it is the right thing to do, but also because you NEVER KNOW who they might know or who they might become. When I first joined networking groups, I was NOT a networking expert or speaker on the topic of networking. Some people showed less respect for me because my profession in the transportation industry didn't seem to match theirs as an attorney or accountant. But I earned their respect over time, and learned to show respect to others regardless of their position in life.

Respect everyone…always. These tips and this book are based on ethical and humanist principles. It is the right thing to show respect to everyone. You might disagree with them, not think that they are highly competent, or younger and less experienced. Nonetheless, show respect to them.

STORY - YOUNG PROFESSIONALS FOR 15 MINUTES

I was asked to give a 15 minute presentation with no compensation to a group of young professionals. My initial thought was "No pay, young audience, only 15 minutes." However…it was a wonderful group of future leaders with whom I connected very strongly. I made several very strong connections at the meeting who responded to me very positively, and got other speaking opportunities based on how well it went. By overcoming my initial perceptions and bias, I treated it with full respect and not only gave my best, but learned a lot in the process and benefited greatly over the long run.

TIP #11 - BE YOURSELF

Many people have the mistaken belief that in order to be successful in networking they have to be a back slapping hand shaking ever smiling glad handing joke telling extrovert. Though extroverts have a slight advantage in social situations, especially in large groups, you can still succeed if you are shy or introverted. Above all, BE YOURSELF. Don't try to conform to some idea of the "ideal networker".

Be honest, be genuine and proud of who you are and where you are from. This concept applies to your age, level of education, profession and socioeconomic status. You can and will be successful if you are true to yourself (and follow the other TIPS).

To quote Dr. Seuss, "Be who you are because people who mind don't matter and people who matter don't mind." Don't be hesitant to express yourself, as that may be the reason people connect with you.

TIP #12 - FOLLOW UP

Networking begins with a greeting, handshake and probable exchange of business cards. All of those elements are important beginnings in the networking process. However, it is what you do in terms of follow-up that truly builds the relationships so they become fruitful.

FOLLOW-UP can take many forms: an e-mail, an invitation to become a LinkedIn connection, an article, newsletter or a phone call. As the world changes rapidly, we have seen the phone and hand written thank you notes be replaced by social media and texting. If you follow up appropriately and regularly (this varies from situation to situation) you are more likely to remain front of mind. If you don't follow up, you will squander the opportunity that networking has offered to you.

Poor or non follow-up will lose not only the referral partners, but the possible business opportunities.

TIP #13 - STAY ON CONSISTENT CHANNELS WITH OTHERS

Everyone has a preferred channel of communication. Examples are: in person, telephone, e-mail, social media and texting. Often people are very clear about the channel that they are most likely to utilize. Some of this "channel preference" is generational. Baby boomers and older often prefer the telephone (even specifying "land line") over e-mail or texting. Millennials and younger tend to eschew more traditional channels (like handwritten notes) and prefer texting and social media.

Pay attention to the channel preference of people you meet in networking, and try to respond in their preferred channel. The channels are continually changing, and you should be flexible in order to stay current. With the continuous advancement of technology, we cannot forget that the ultimate goal is to CONNECT.

TIP #14 - BE PREPARED FOR TROIKAS AND SMALL GROUP MEETINGS

Today we are able to prepare ourselves for meetings like never before. We can do research on others through Google and LinkedIn that allow us to learn much in advance about a person's work experience, educational background and other pertinent data. DO YOUR HOMEWORK! People will be impressed when you arrive at meetings and already know the basics of their business and experience. When you actually get to the meeting, always be a good listener, and ask others such questions as "What is a good referral for you?" and "Who do you want to meet or need to know?" Pay attention to the responses, and try to respond as quickly and appropriately as possible to the information that is presented. If you really want to impress others (and be a good networker), have some suggestions about referrals, introductions and trusted advice when you arrive at the troika.

Another great question is "what would have to happen during this meeting for you to walk away thinking it was an overwhelming success?"

TIP #15 - GIVING EFFECTIVE REFERRALS

There are two major schools of thought on giving referrals. The first and more traditional is to give three referrals in all cases. In fact, some professions have mandated this practice. If you don't have to give more than one referral, and you have one person who is far and away the most qualified and appropriate, you can and should refer that person with a high level of enthusiasm.

If you know numerous people in a particular profession or specialty, you should refer the person who is most appropriate for the request. For example, if someone is looking for a financial advisor who specializes in working with middle-aged women in the Long Beach area, and you know someone who is qualified in that area, then that would be the best referral.

Writing an e-mail to both the referral source and the person requesting the referral has become a common and effective practice. That way the person getting the referral can offer thanks to the referral source and indicate their interest in the case by a Reply All response.

Ultimately, there must be the MOTIVATION to make a referral, a call to action based on some tipping point. For some people it is natural and abundant (they refer frequently and enthusiastically). For others, it is like pulling teeth. Keep in mind that referrals and introductions are at the core of effective networking practices. Learn to be proactive and develop a "referral mindset."

TIP #16 - REFERRAL ETIQUETTE BASICS

When you receive a referral, the very first thing to do is to thank the person who made the referral to you. If you are instructed by the referring person to contact the potential client, do so immediately. Set up an appointment in a timely manner. Always act in a professional manner. If the client asks for additional referrals to people in related fields, it is best to check with the original referral source to see if they want to make that secondary referral and any additional referrals.

Above all, do the best job you can possibly do to be fully worthy of the referral. Reciprocate if possible. If appropriate, take the referral source out to lunch or dinner to express your gratitude. Thoughtful gifts (like a bottle of wine or gift card) are also great tokens of appreciation. Old school touches like handwritten notes can be very powerful and will differentiate you from most people who don't send them.

TIP #17 - USING KNOWLEDGE OF YOUR BIORHYTHMS TO MAXIMIZE PRODUCTIVITY

Everyone has a slightly different circadian rhythm, which leads them to be more alert and productive at certain times of day. At one extreme are "larks" or "early birds" who prefer to wake up very early and go to bed early. At the other end of the spectrum are "night owls" who tend to wake up later and stay up later. This phenomenon has a great impact on our attendance and alertness at networking meetings and social events.

Many networking groups meet in the morning, which favors the early risers. If you tend not to like to wake up early, then you should look for groups that have lunch or evening meetings. Other variations are times when we are less alert like midday or late afternoon. Learn and pay attention to your own circadian rhythms so that you can maximize your effectiveness in networking groups and situations.

Don't be a biorhythm bully. If everyone else wants to have lunch at 12 noon, don't insist on 1:30 because it is convenient for you.

TIP #18 - BALANCE IN PERSON AND SOCIAL MEDIA NETWORKING

There is no substitute for meeting others in person, face to face. Show up, get involved and get to know others over time. Social media allows you to continue to build your network beyond in person networking. Effective networking utilizes a combination of in person meetings and events, and the prudent use of social media.

In terms of social media, you can also balance the business aspects with the personal ones. LinkedIn (business) and Facebook (personal) allow you to do both. Of course, you can use social media any time of day, and in person networking is more time limited. It is thoughtful and useful to LIKE and positively comment on others' posts, birthdays and other milestones mentioned in social media. Make your comments personal and thoughtful. They will be appreciated by others. It is great to make meaningful social media posts, but over posting is annoying to others and has diminishing returns.

TIP #19 - DON'T RUSH PEOPLE IN CONVERSATION

When you are in conversation with others, don't rush them. Be patient, let them finish their thoughts, sentences and stories. If you are at a networking event, don't be in a hurry to mingle, especially when you are in a meaningful and productive conversation. People appreciate and LIKE others who allow them to complete their points without feeling rushed.

Networking is NOT speed dating, and one of the biggest mistakes people make is to try to talk to as many people as possible, and end up not really talking to anyone at all.

TIP #20 - ADMIT YOUR MISTAKES

When you make a mistake, are late to a meeting or the completion of a project, ADMIT IT. You will gain respect and be better off in the long run if you simply apologize and admit your mistake or shortcoming. When apologizing, do so without qualifying the apology such as "I am sorry I was late but this meeting was too early for me."

A simple, direct admission goes a long way to building your credibility and will strengthen rather than weaken you.

TIP #21 - DON'T INTERRUPT OTHERS

Be polite in conversation. Don't ever interrupt others when they are in the middle of talking. Let them finish their thoughts. This tip is a corollary to Tip #19. People really appreciate it when they are talking with someone who is polite and willing to let them speak until completion. Even when you are excited and think you know exactly what someone is going to say, resist the temptation to finish their sentences for them.

TIP #22 - HAVE GOOD TABLE MANNERS

When you are sharing a meal with others, have good table manners. Try to eat at a similar pace as others. Don't talk with your mouth full of food. Wipe your mouth if you have food on it. If you are eating family style, don't overindulge.

TIP #23 - SAY THANK YOU FREQUENTLY

Thank you is perhaps the most powerful thing you can say. Show gratitude often and sincerely. Whenever someone does anything for you, thank them promptly. If you appreciate something another has done for you, make sure they know that you do.

Thank you's can be done on any channel: phone, gift, e-mail, text. The important thing is that you are generous in your expressions of appreciation.

STORY - GIFT GIVING AS GRATITUDE

When someone tells you about one of their preferences or tastes, pay attention to it. Sue was a very important client, and I wanted to give her a gift in appreciation of all of the business she had given me over the years. I knew that she drank wine, and thought that giving her a couple of bottles of wine would be appropriate. I asked her whether she preferred red or white, and she said white wine was her preference. Knowing a bit about wine, I asked if she preferred chardonnay or sauvignon blanc. She indicated that she had a strong preference for California chardonnays. I did some research, and found a high quality California chardonnay and gave her a couple of bottles. She was VERY thankful, and this gesture further cemented our already strong relationship. It pays to listen carefully and to be thoughtful.

TIP #24 - BE PRUDENT IN DISCUSSION TOPICS

You should be aware of the risks of talking about things like politics, religion or sex. The main risk is polarizing others. If you want to have a larger, diverse network, I recommend staying away from controversial topics. This applies not only to conversation, but also to e-mail and social media postings.

You are obviously free to express yourself and your passions, but be aware that whenever you express them, there is the risk of alienating someone with an opposing view. In order to have a wider, more diverse network, keep your opinions to yourself or express them in a more appropriate venue. If you are interested more in freely stating your opinions than in building a wide business network in terms of age, gender, ethnicity, religion, and political persuasion, then you have more latitude to express more controversial opinions. Thus, the purpose of your networking will determine the scope of your expression of opinions, especially controversial ones.

The main exception to this principle is when you really know someone and know that you share particular opinions or beliefs. In that case, talking about something can be a positive bonding experience.

TIP #25 - DON'T MONOPOLIZE CONVERSATIONS OR HOLD PEOPLE CAPTIVE

Be aware of how interested people actually are in what you are saying. Less is more. Don't monopolize discussions. Know when to stop, or check in with people and see if they are really interested when you are going on and on and on and on. And furthermore blah blah blah.

Watch for body language that might indicate that others have had enough of your verbal rampage. When they say "I gotta go" don't continue to talk. Find ways to reduce what you say and how long you speak at one time. Perhaps have a friend time you to see how long you might be speaking. Work on being more concise. Rambling is annoying to others, and should be avoided. Having said that, I WILL STOP.

TIP #26 - DON'T BE A CLOSE TALKER: RESPECT PEOPLE'S PERSONAL SPACE

Be aware to how close you get to people when you are talking to them. Personal space varies from culture to culture, but generally speaking, people don't like their personal space invaded. Don't be a "close talker." Pay attention to others. If they are backing away from you, it might mean that you are making them uncomfortable. Avoid hugging everyone if you are not certain they want to be hugged, or linger too long with a hug.

TIP #27 - ASK "IS THIS A GOOD TIME TO TALK" WHEN YOU CALL SOMEONE

When you call someone on the phone, ask them if it is a good time to talk before launching into a discussion. If they say NO, then ask when might be a good time. The other technique which is becoming increasing popular is to actually set a specific time for a call. Even when you do that, it is wise and polite to ask "Is it a good time to talk?"

TIP #28 - DON'T FLAKE ON MEETINGS

When you schedule a meeting, SHOW UP as scheduled. Don't flake just because something better came along. There are legitimate reasons for canceling or postponing meetings, but don't do so on a whim. You will lose a lot of credibility and business if you get the reputation as someone who is unreliable.

It is also useful to send reminders to others regarding meetings. If you are going to be late or if you get lost, inform the other attendees of your tardiness. Be polite and respectful of others, and they will likely be the same with you.

There are times when you have set up a coffee meeting or lunch, but for some reason just don't want to go. This happens occasionally, and when it does, it is advisable to keep the appointment. By SHOWING UP you might derive a benefit, and more importantly you demonstrate your reliability. People who cancel meetings without a good reason are giving a work sample that is not positive.

TIP #29 - PAYING THE BILL

It has become very common in networking groups to break up into smaller groups called troikas or minis. That is when 3-4 people have a meal together to get to know each other better. When you do that, you have the issue of how to pay the bill. It has become a norm that the bill is split evenly, regardless of what everyone had to eat. Another increasingly acceptable norm is that everyone puts in a credit card instead of cash.

There are some exceptions to this practice. One is when a person obviously eats substantially more (or less) than the others. Another is when some people drink alcohol and others don't. Common sense and fairness should prevail. Another exception is when one person specifically invites another to lunch (or breakfast or dinner) to ask them for something. In that case the inviter should pick up the tab.

TIP #30 - DON'T BE A LOUDMOUTH

Speak at a reasonable level. Don't be loud or obnoxious. If you get consistent feedback that you are too loud, tone it down a bit. A corollary to this is to be sensitive to the ambient noise in a room. If it is too loud, suggest and move to a quieter area.

TIP #31 - ENCOURAGE AND SUPPORT PEOPLE IN YOUR NETWORK COMMUNITY

Be a supporter of others. Encourage people who are going after sales, writing books, or interviewing for a position. You can do this best in person, but today we have the opportunity to LIKE people on many diverse channels. Be sincere in your comments, and remember that the more people you help along the way, the more will be there for you. What goes around definitely comes around!!

TIP #32 - YOU NEVER KNOW

Don't prejudge people and their potential value to you. YOU NEVER KNOW. The younger, less experienced person might be strongly connected to someone you really want to meet. Show respect to everyone, and you will definitely derive value from people who you initially thought were somehow beneath you in status. Be humble and open-minded, and it will pay huge dividends.

TIP #33 - IF YOU ARE A GOOD STORY TELLER, TELL STORIES

Stories can be fantastic ways to communicate. Some people are more gifted and inclined to tell compelling stories. If you like telling stories and are good at them, tell them. However, be aware of time and others' responses and possible time constraints. Be aware of who you have told specific stories to, and don't repeat the same story to the same person.

TIP #34 - DON'T PUBLICLY CRITICIZE OR DEMEAN OTHERS

In a networking situation, don't criticize or demean others. Be kind and try to say positive things about others. If you really have a problem with someone, you can share it privately to a close friend or associate. Like my mom said, "If you don't have anything nice to say about someone, don't say anything."

TIP #35 - HAVE GOOD HYGIENE

Shower, use deodorant, brush your teeth, look in the mirror prior to leaving your house, and be clean. Have good hygiene. Be aware of yourself, your look, your attire, your smell. If you are going to pile up your plate with onions, garlic and curry, it is probably best not to be a close talker. This area is all part of your personal brand and the impression you make on others.

TIP #36 - CAPITALIZE ON COMMONALITIES

Try to find common ground with others like: hobbies, schools, hometown, television show, travel, animals, gardening. When someone mentions anything that you can connect with, make the connection. If there is a name mentioned or you have a social media connection in common, don't hesitate to bring it up to establish some common ground.

Work to build bridges, not burn them. There will be plenty of instances where there will be differences. Focus more on what you have in common, not where you differ with others.

STORY - HIGH SCHOOL FOOTBALL

I had an appointment in my moving business, and the potential customer looked vaguely familiar. I asked him where he was from (because I had a hunch) and he said he was from Pasadena. I asked him if he played football there, and he affirmed that he did. I told him that I also played football at Pasadena High School (go Bulldogs!!). We made a connection, and he was so taken by this common ground that he told me he would award me the contract on the basis of that connection. It is advisable to ask the other person if you think there is a common ground. If I hadn't asked, my chances of securing the business would have been less.

TIP #37 - CALL PEOPLE BY NAME

Call people by name when you talk to them. Try to learn and remember people's name. Don't use the excuse that you aren't good with names!! Pay attention and use the name in conversation which helps memory. This may seem like a small thing, but it really does have a major impact in making positive connections with others. Calling people by their name is an extremely powerful tool to connect with others.

TIP #38 - WIDEN THE CIRCLE BY MAKING INTRODUCTIONS

When you are at a networking event or social gathering and you are standing around and people are mingling, there will be situations where someone will walk into your space and conversation. If you know them, introduce them without interrupting the flow of the conversation to the person or people you are talking to and widen the circle. If their conversation continues, this can give you the opportunity to mingle with others if you choose to do so.

TIP #39 - BE FLEXIBLE

Try to remain flexible in all areas of your life, but especially in terms of scheduling meetings. People appreciate others who are flexible and willing to compromise. If someone needs to change the time of a meeting or call and it can be done, you are well advised to be willing to change the time (or place).

TIP #40 - THERE ARE TIMES NOT TO NETWORK

Although networking is a way of life, there are times when it is better to relax, enjoy the time you are spending with others, and not to network at all. Some of these are:

- when you are at a religious ceremony
- when you are shopping at a store
- when you are at your significant other's event
- when you are told not to network
- when someone seems very upset about something (timing is EVERYTHING)
- when an event is specifically on a topic that does not involve you

Common sense should prevail, and often it is better to have someone ask you what you do than to thrust your business card into their hand.

TIP #41 - BE AWARE OF TIME

It is important to be aware of time and to respect others' time. The starting point is to have a sense of how long 1 minute, 5 minutes and 1 hour really are. A lunch might be somewhere between an hour upward, and you should take cues and get a sense of how long a meeting will last.

Every location, occupation and person allots a different amount of time for a meal or coffee meeting. Learn some of the norms by asking questions, but remain flexible. If you get the sense that the conversation is going REALLY well and that the feeling is mutual, it is advisable not to curtail the flow by arbitrary time limits. You can ask the other person "How are you doing with time?"

TIP #42 - USING SOCIAL MEDIA INVOLVES COMMUNICATION

In using social media such as LinkedIn and Facebook, the real value is in communication. It is not enough to sign up, create a profile and wait for people to give you business. You need to communicate. This can take the form of the following:

- status updates
- sharing interesting articles
- e-mails through the sites
- recommendations and endorsements
- making introductions
- doing research on people or companies
- asking for introductions when appropriate

In order to get something out of social media, you must actively engage with others on a regular basis. It is not just about you, but more about them. Pay attention, respond and deepen the connections. Find common ground and comment on it. Use social media as a springboard to face-to-face communication.

TIP #43 - IF I SAY MY NAME IS BILL, DON'T CALL ME WILLIAM

Call people by the name they prefer to be called. If someone introduces themselves as David, call him David. If at some point you notice a few people calling him Dave, ask him what he prefers. Shortening names can be a sensitive area, especially when people are adamant about being called a specific version of their name.

As you get to know people and are more comfortable and less formal with them, it is likely acceptable to use diminutives (Bill for William, Sue for Susan). People introduce themselves a certain way for a reason, and it is best to respect it rather than deciding what you want to call them.

Everyone makes a decision to put a certain name on their business card or correspondence. They do it for some reason. Formal names, nicknames of preference, use of middle initials or full middle names, titles and trade names are all utilized in varying forms. In some cases these are the names that people prefer. In other cases they don't really go by that name. If in doubt, ask the name of preference.

TIP #44 - MEET THE CONNECTORS AND GET THEM TO LIKE YOU

There are people who are very well connected, and who also like to connect others. When you meet a connector, and they take a liking to you, there is a good chance that they will be willing to introduce you to people they already know.

It is a lot easier to meet someone through a "warm" connection than to cold call them to try to set up a meeting. If you go back to the basic networking paradigm, you will see how important the LIKE stage is. The stronger the liking, the more chance of getting an introduction.

You might also be judged (positively or negatively) based on your connections. Often people are accepted (or rejected) primarily on the basis of their associations.

TIP #45- ALWAYS BE SURE TO CARRY BUSINESS CARDS

Always carry plenty of business cards to networking meetings and mixers, and have them handy to give to others. The business card exchange has been a staple of the networking process for many years, though it might be waning a bit due to ecological concerns related to paper conservation.

Hand your business card to people, presented so it can be read. When receiving a business card, study it briefly rather than quickly stuffing it into your pocket. You can photograph the cards and put them into your database, or request a LinkedIn connection based on the collection of business cards.

It is wise to put your cards in multiple places so that you always access some as needed.

TIP #46 - BE A HARD WORKER IN COMMITTEES

When you volunteer to work on a committee or project, be a hard and diligent worker. Your involvement is an important work sample which can determine whether or not someone makes referrals or introductions to you. Honor all commitments in a timely manner. If for some reason you are going to be late in meeting deadlines, inform others about your intentions to complete all promised tasks and likely completion date.

In addition to being prompt in completion, do a quality job in everything you do. Be a team player in all cases. Don't overstate your accomplishments. Leave that to others.

STORY - BEAM ME UP SCOTTY

Scotty was a young aspiring accountant who wanted to work at a major accounting firm. He was working at a smaller firm, and at one point was asked if he wanted to assist with a large charity event. He accepted that role, and did an outstanding job working on that event. A senior partner in a large firm noticed Scotty's work ethic and competence. A position opened at a major firm, and though Scotty was one of many applicants, he secured the position largely because of his exemplary work on the charity event. Remember that every time you volunteer for something that your work will be noticed.

TIP #47 - STAY ENGAGED IN CONVERSATIONS

Be a good and focused conversationalist. Don't get distracted by the "glowing rectangle" that is your smart phone. It is wise to put your phone on vibrate when you are in a meeting. People like to know that you are fully engaged with them, and not easily distracted by phone calls, text messages or other things.

If you absolutely must be available for phone calls during a troika or meeting, make the other person aware of that in advance and sincerely apologize for any inconvenience.

TIP #48 - RESPECT EXISTING GROUPS THAT YOU VISIT AS A GUEST

When you visit a group as a guest, show respect for the existing group. It takes time to be assimilated into an existing group or clique. Get to know all of the members, and NEVER speak negatively about anyone in that group. You never know the nature of existing relationships.

Be observant and ask about any norms of the group you are visiting. Don't impose your own values when you are a visitor.

TIP #49 - ENJOY YOUR HOBBIES WITH OTHERS FOR PURELY PERSONAL REASONS

If you have a hobby like riding a bicycle, hiking or playing golf, you can possibly enjoy these activities with members of your networking group or business community. I recommend that when you do these activities you keep business conversations to a minimum. You can just enjoy the activity and converse with others as friends rather than business associates. By doing so, you can build very strong relationships and even develop some genuine friendships.

Always show good sportsmanship and a respect for others and individual differences. There is more than one way of playing games and doing things. It is okay to be competitive, but always be a gracious winner and loser.

TIP #50 - STAY IN TOUCH WITH PEOPLE IN YOUR NETWORK

Meeting people is only one step, albeit an important one, in the overall networking process. Staying in touch over time is an even more important step in the process. It is really quite simple. If you don't stay in touch with people they will eventually forget about you, and you might be replaced by people who do stay in touch. The exact amount to stay in touch will vary from person to person and situation to situation, but there are many ways to do so.

Phone calls, the "old school" way, still works. Other methods are e-mail, social media and a newsletter. If you are in networking groups, SHOW UP and show up consistently. Regular attendance is one of the most fundamental principles of networking.

Contact management systems like Constant Contact or Act are useful to manage your database of contacts.

TIP #51 - REVEAL INTERESTING THINGS ABOUT YOURSELF: SELF-DISCLOSURE CAN DEEPEN RELATIONSHIPS

One way to deepen existing relationships is by revealing interesting personal things about yourself. Self-disclosure (within reason) tends to deepen relationships. As you get to know people, there is a tendency to talk about more personal matters and events in your life. When you do that kind of sharing it humanizes you more than strictly business conversations. Though potentially distracting, self-disclosure could uncover empathy in you or others or the revelation of a common experience.

TIP #52 - DON'T PREJUDGE OR STEREOTYPE OTHERS

Perception of self and others is an important component of the networking process. Make an effort to remain open minded about others, and not to prejudge or stereotype them based on their age, ethnicity, profession or other aspect of their lives.

You might find out something about their previous career, educational background, hobbies, talents or other experiences. Don't assume that you know everything about someone. Be humble in your assessments of others, and remain open to new and possibly revealing information.

STORY - SORRY, BUT WE CAN'T LET YOU IN BECAUSE YOU ARE JUST A VENDOR

About ten years ago a man who was in business development for a transportation company tried to join a networking group. He was denied membership, and was informed that the primary reason was that he was "just a vendor" and didn't meet the membership qualification of being a "trusted advisor." Though disappointed, he accepted that decision and went on with his work. A couple of years later a member of that exclusive group told him that he should have been admitted, and lobbied on his behalf. He was accepted by a Group Leader who said to him, "I want you in my group. It should be the person not the profession that determines membership." After being accepted into the group, he worked hard to prove his worth. He got involved as a member of the executive committee of that group. He became versed and then an expert on the networking process, using his background in psychology to form his ideas and wrote a well regarded book on the topic. He began training and coaching in networking and business development, became a group leader, and eventually became President of Bruin Professionals. That person is me, and that is my story. It is living proof to not judge a book by its cover, and that hard work can overcome just about anything.

TIP #53- COLLABORATE WITH OTHERS WHEN POSSIBLE

Sometimes in networking groups we meet others we initially consider to be competitors who do exactly what we do. In some cases that is true, and collaboration is unlikely or impossible. However, in many cases people we might have considered to be competitors can actually become great allies and people with whom we can successfully collaborate.

As you learn about others, be open to the possibility of collaborating with them. Collaboration is usually based on a high level of trust as a prerequisite. Your competitor can ultimately become a trusted ally, especially when they get busy and might need your help or might refer to you.

STORY - TWO RESIDENTIAL REAL ESTATE BROKERS DECIDE TO JOIN FORCES

Sheila Rose, a broker-associate with Berkshire Hathaway and Andrea Best, a broker with Nourmand & Associates, are members in the same chapter of a networking group called Bruin Professionals, which is part of the Alumni Association of UCLA. They are of a similar age and level of experience. What happened is that in the process of attending a large number of networking meetings in the same chapter, and being members of the executive committee of that chapter, they became friends. They gradually realized that it might make sense to collaborate, even though they worked for different companies. So what they did was to brand themselves as partners for any business that came directly from Bruin Professionals. They stopped being competitors and became a viable team. This partnership enhanced both of their businesses. People in their mutual network had an easier decision, and didn't have to select one over the other.

TIP #54 - HOW TO ESCAPE RAMBLERS

I have been asked on numerous occasions, "How can I best get away from someone who goes on and on and on and on?" This is actually a very tough question. First of all, it is important to be polite and not to summarily cut people off. But in some cases people do hold others hostage by rambling without sensitivity to time constraints and whether the other person is actually interested in what they are saying.

So what should you do when you are a "victim"? There are a couple of possible solutions. One is to wait for a pause and then assertively and forcefully tell the "rambler" that you really need to leave. Another tactic is to respectfully and carefully interrupt the other person and tell them that you are sorry, but you have to leave. You can also use a diplomatic preventative method by setting time limits in advance of a conversation.

TIP #55 - KEEP YOUR BRAND SIMPLE AND CLEAR

Branding has become increasingly important in today's complex world. It can make or break the success of individuals and organizations. Keep your brand simple and understandable. Even if you do more than one thing, most people can only deal with one specialization at a time. When you are giving your elevator speech, it is preferable to keep it to a single clear message.

You can differentiate yourself with a unique or clever tag line or specialty, and people will tend to remember you and what you do.

There are exceptions to this principle. For example, if you do two or more distinct things, you can emphasize one of them and allude to the others.

TIP #56- BE GENUINELY INTERESTED AND REMAIN CURIOUS ABOUT OTHERS

In conversation, develop an attitude of being genuinely interested and curious about others. Don't be afraid to ask questions, though some types of questions are inappropriate. Health, politics, sex, religion and humor are all potentially dangerous, but in some cases those same subjects are the basis of a connection.

By being interested, you will tend to be a better listener. Pay attention and make an effort to remember pertinent information. You don't have to remember everything, but try to use some of the information in conversation to aid retention of it.

TIP #57 - BE TOLERANT OF INDIVIDUAL AND CULTURAL DIFFERENCES

There are no rules here, but you should try to have tolerance (the more the better) for differences among people. This can really refer to most anything like: pace, circadian rhythm, eating choices, speed of driving. It could also refer to regional and generational differences among people. To be a versatile networker, tolerance truly helps, especially when you want to widen your network.

Being tolerant does not mean that you have to give up or deny your beliefs. However, if you really need to state your beliefs constantly, you will reduce the size and breadth of your potential network. The topics you discuss, the stories you tell, the context, the intention of the meeting, the location, the time frame and many other things differ from conversation to conversation.

It will serve you well to be observant and aware of this, and to become versatile in your conversational skills. Great networkers are aware of this, and are able to connect with a very wide variety of people. They are able to be comfortable with people in different age groups, professions, religion, political persuasion, university affiliation and other variables.

It starts with awareness of differences, some obvious, some subtle. It also takes tolerance, flexibility and verbal skills which are likely to be developed over a long period of time. Emotional intelligence really helps, but you can learn the basic skills without being very high in emotional intelligence. Be willing to learn from another person's perspective.

TIP #58 - PRACTICE RANDOM ACTS OF CONGRATULATION

In today's world so deeply influenced by social media, you will have many opportunities to congratulate others for promotions, getting hired, work anniversaries, birthdays and other accomplishments. If you have the time and inclination, seize some of those to make a thoughtful "touch".

In offering these salvos, it is important to personalize them for increased meaning. So instead of merely "Congratulations" or Like you could say "Congratulations Bob on your new job. I'm sure you will do a great job there."

TIP #59 - BE HUMBLE ABOUT YOUR ACCOMPLISHMENTS AND SKILLS

Don't ever be a braggart. Even though you might be great and highly skilled, let others do your bragging for you. Be humble. It mighty be tempting to toot your own horn, but trust that your skills and accomplishments will be recognized eventually.

TIP #60 - GROUP SIZE CAN HAVE A HUGE IMPACT ON CONVERSATION

Group size is a major determinant of human interaction. A dyad, or two people, allows the most intimate type of conversation. It is most desirable for introverts or shy people, and allows the fewest potential interruptions. The troika, or three people, allows more diverse interaction. However, there is increasing possibility of one person dominating the conversation. As you add people, there is decreasing likelihood of the ideal of a one to one dyad.

When you really want to have a direct conversation with a person, stick to one to one. If you want more of an interchange, then increasing the number of participants is desirable. More people can make for a more diverse exchange of ideas. In sum, there are advantages and disadvantages in different group sizes.

TIP #61 - SEATING ARRANGEMENTS CAN HAVE MAJOR INFLUENCE ON COMMUNICATION

The way you are seated has an impact, sometimes a major one, on communication. All participants should be comfortable and able to hear one another. Face to face communication is best, but not always possible. When you are having a meal with three people, a round table is ideal but a booth is acceptable. With three people, you have to decide where everyone sits. Factors like noise, weather and proximity to others should also be considered. Try to find a quiet corner in a restaurant where you can be easily heard and understood.

TIP #62 - SELF-PERCEPTION CAN BE DIFFERENT FROM HOW OTHERS SEE YOU

We all have an image of who we are. We might see ourselves as agreeable, flexible, helpful or determined. Others might perceive us in many different ways. It is important to know that our own self-image might not match what various others think of us. When people tell us what they think of us, and it doesn't match our own self-image, we can either try to correct them or consider that we might actually present ourselves in ways different from what we think of ourselves. It is best not to be defensive or argumentative in this regard, but to consider alternative perceptions, especially when more than one person tells us a particular thing.

There is how we see ourselves, how others see us, and reality.

TIP #63 - EFFECTIVE NETWORKING TAKES TIME: BE PATIENT

In order to be really effective in networking, it takes time. You have to build relationships and trust. Don't rush people or expect them to give you referrals right away. As stated previously, find ways to give and make yourself memorable. Brand yourself in your elevator speech, and when you get in smaller groups, you can discuss some additional variations on what you can do.

Sometimes it takes several meetings for others to REALLY know who you are and what you do. Don't give up on networking before you have given it a chance to work. Remember that it takes time to build mutually beneficial relationships.

STORY - ASK FOR HELP FROM EXISTING NETWORK

Robin had been the leader of a networking group for several years, and had built very strong and enduring relationships with the members of her group. She had been working in public relations and her business partner announced that he was going to retire. She found herself in a dilemma of not having a job, and that created a good deal of anxiety for her. She decided that she was going to announce publicly to her group that she needed help and was looking for ideas. Someone suggested that she seek employment from the networking organization. She was hired, and found the new job to be a great fit for her. This story illustrates how we can use existing relationships to secure assistance in various areas of our lives.

TIP #64- RESPECT CONFIDENTIALITY

When someone tells you something in confidence, or your professional ethics demand confidentiality, respect it completely. Don't ever share information that was told to you in confidence - EVER!! Professions like law, financial management or psychotherapy have very strict rules of confidentiality. However, even if you are in a field without such strict ethical rules, you should be careful not to share information that is intended to be private. People tell you things in confidence because they trust you; don't abuse that trust!!

This principle extends to public testimonials, as much as you might want to thank someone for a referral. If in doubt, ask the person if it is okay to mention something that could be confidential or privileged information.

TIP #65 - ENGAGE YOUR NETWORK CONSISTENTLY AND APPROPRIATELY

In order to maintain a vital and productive network, you must engage it consistently. The engagement can be through social media, a useful newsletter, e-mail messages or other channels. Don't overdo it or become overexposed. As stated earlier, people will forget about you if you don't stay in touch. However, they will want to forget about you if you over-share. Engaging your network is done through your original posts and messages, and by responding to the communication of others.

This all takes time, and the busier you are, the more selective you need to be about your posting.

TIP #66- DON'T BE A BLABBER MOUTH

Don't talk too much, especially about sensitive or confidential subjects. Think before you speak. Everyone has some type of "censor" that filters thoughts before they become words and sentences. Use that censor and be prudent in what you say publicly. In general, listen more than you speak.

TIP #67 - IF YOU GO WIDE, YOU STILL NEED TO FOLLOW UP

If and when you take your network wide through social media, you must remember to follow up with the people that you reach. There is minimal value in widening your network if you neglect to follow up. Follow-up can take various forms, such as: wishing Happy Birthday, LinkedIn endorsements, Likes, commenting on their posts, sending relevant articles or just an occasional touch of some sort.

TIP #68 - FIRST IMPRESSIONS MIGHT BE WRONG: GIVE SECOND CHANCES

When we meet people, they create some kind of impression. Their work also creates an impression. Sometimes first impressions turn out to be 100% representative of who the person becomes in your experience. However...there are many times when our first impressions were erroneous or proven wrong by subsequent experiences.

On one hand, you should trust your judgment, your gut, your instinct and/or your intuition. But be willing to modify your opinion based on subsequent positive experiences. You never know...or do you?

STORY - DOUBTFUL ABOUT DANNY

I met Danny about ten years ago. He was a member of my networking group. Danny is an accountant, very bright and well educated. My initial perception of Danny was that he was arrogant and egotistical. He left our group for awhile, then returned. Danny was always friendly, but I kept my distance because of my initial impression. We had lunch in a troika, and my perceptions turned out to be incorrect. Danny was perfectly delightful, and gave me a fantastic referral. I am grateful that I didn't let my first impression remain permanent. I was wrong about Danny, and very happy that I changed that impression.

TIP #69 - EMPATHY IS A GREAT NETWORKING ASSET

Empathy is the ability to accurately identify and understand the world of another. This skill has wide ranging value in networking, and can lead to instant connections. As you listen intently to others, and understand their feelings and perspective (or have a similar one), share that understanding to determine if it is accurate. As your range of experience increases you will have the ability to empathize more widely. If you are comfortable with another person, have genuine empathy for their situation, don't hesitate to share it.

STORY - EMPATHY PAYS OFF

I met Randy about ten years ago. He is an attorney, and one day he asked if I wanted to go on a walk with him after a networking meeting. I said yes, not knowing or caring about his motivation (I love to walk!). He proceeded to share information and his sadness over a recent separation from his wife of many years. Having been through divorce, I was able to empathize with him. Our conversation had NOTHING to do with networking, and was totally personal. My intentions were totally related to being a friend when someone was hurting. Randy has become a good friend, and in addition to our friendship, he makes referrals to me on a regular basis. I doubt if our relationship would have developed that way it did without that conversation on our walk. Empathy is very powerful in building relationships. If you identify with the world of another, don't hesitate to communicate that connection.

TIP #70 - IF YOUR BUSINESS IS SPECIFIC AND REGIONAL, GO DEEP

The decision about whether to take your network wide or deep is often easily determined by the following situation. If your business is primarily very specific and within a local area, it is wiser to go DEEP than wide. There is probably not much value in going wide to areas that you cannot service in your business.

TIP #71 - GO WIDE IF YOUR REACH IS LARGER

When you have a more general business and are looking to build a network in a larger region, go WIDE. It is also prudent to take your network wide when you are open to a wider spectrum of contacts. In other words, when you don't really know who you could network with, then going wider makes sense. For example, my relocation business can be practiced virtually anywhere, and referrals can come from wide and far. Therefore, I have gone wide with my network and garnered referrals from many geographic areas.

TIP #72- GET TO KNOW MORE ABOUT PEOPLE YOU ALREADY KNOW

Networking is an ongoing process of getting to know people better and better, deeper and deeper over time. For example, you might learn that they like dogs, find out about the breed of dog, learn about the dog shows, and so on. You will learn about their upbringing, their families, their interests and many more things. The more you know people, the more possibilities there are for sharing business. Take notes to aid in memory of significant information. You don't have to remember everything, just the important stuff.

TIP #73 - AGE IS OFTEN DECEPTIVE

There is often a large real and imagined age difference in networking settings. It is not necessary (or even desirable) to ask other people's age. But if they offer it, be aware of how age differences might affect interactions. I have experienced many situations where others are highly accomplished despite their relatively young age. Additionally, I have met people who appeared much younger than their actual age. Thus, age can be deceptive and more than meets the eye. It can truly be a state of mind.

TIP #74 - SUCCESS IN NETWORKING TAKES PATIENCE

Simply stated, relationships take time to develop. Additionally, some people will not make a referral or introduction until they have a very high level of trust in another person. Be patient. Too often people quit networking groups prematurely, without giving relationships time to develop. Serving on committees and volunteering will accelerate this process, but patience is still very important. Don't rush people. Let them get to know you.

TIP #75 - PICK UP THE PHONE

The phone conversation still has a pivotal place in business and personal communication, though it is ever changing. Especially in the case of controversial or contentious conversations, or things that are complicated, phone conversations are preferable to e-mails, texting or social media communication. It is too easy to misconstrue subtle emotional shadings in e-mail. Don't write e-mails when you are upset or angry. It is preferable to file it as a draft and revisit it later to determine if you should send it. When in doubt, PICK UP THE PHONE. Don't resort to e-mail, especially group e-mails when you really need a direct one to one communication that has nuance to it. If the situation is really complicated, an in person meeting is even more useful than talking on the phone.

TIP #76 - BE CAREFUL OR AVOID DUAL RELATIONSHIPS

A dual relationship is something like being a friend and a boss, a client and member of a social group, or any time you have more than one possibly conflicting relationship with the same person. Sometimes this is unavoidable, but often you might become friends with a business associate. The problem often arises when you have to make a possibly uncomfortable decision, or let the friendship get in the way of your decision.

TIP #77 - TRY TO MAKE OTHERS FEEL COMFORTABLE

One of the keys to being likable is to be able to make others feel comfortable around you. You do this by being a good listener, genuinely interested in what they have to say. It is also important to be non-judgmental. When people are comfortable around you, they are more likely to trust you and share things like their feelings and information. By being relaxed and receptive, you will tend to draw people toward you.

TIP #78 - BE FLEXIBLE

Try to keep an open mind, and remain flexible in both your thinking and your behavior. Even though you may want things to go a certain way, it is useful to be open to the inevitable changes that occur among people. People will appreciate your flexibility and be more likely to want to work with you.

TIP #79 - BE CONCISE IN YOUR E-MAIL COMMUNICATION

In today's busy world with the massive amount of electronic communication, be clear, concise and to the point. Don't ramble or ask too many questions in a single e-mail. People are busy and want to know not only what you are trying to communicate, but also exactly what responses you are seeking.

TIP #80 - IF YOU ARE INTROVERTED/SHY, SET UP ONE TO ONE MEETINGS

If you are an introvert/shy, you probably don't love or even like large gatherings. Perhaps they are not ideal for you to network. In fact, they can seem downright intimidating to many people. You can still attend such larger events, but where you will get most benefit and mileage from networking is in smaller, preferably one to one, meetings. You can do this by setting up coffee meetings, and being clear that it is a one to one and not a group meeting.

STORY - WHEN A TROIKA BECOMES A DYAD

In late 2008 when I was in the process of writing Connecting: Beyond the Name Tag, I had a troika (3 way meeting) scheduled with the late Gordon Gregory and one other person. Gordon was then the Managing Director of ProVisors, a very large networking group with over 3,000 members. At the time I was in need of support and research data for my book. As it turned out the third person canceled and I was able to have a one on one meeting with THE MAN.

I prepared meticulously for the meeting, so that I could use it to pitch my book to Gordon. As it turned out, he was quite receptive and gave me about 10 names of people who I could interview for my upcoming book. I used Gordon's name and every one of them set up a meeting with me. The interviews helped immeasurably in the completion of my book.

This example is important for a couple of reasons. First, it illustrates the potential difference between a meeting of three and a meeting of two people. Secondly, it points up the power of using someone's name to get a meeting. Finally, that private meeting was hugely instrumental in helping me develop my book, and Gordon's support was critical to the success of the book.

TIP #81- YOU CAN ENHANCE YOUR NETWORK BY RELATIONSHIPS WITH FAMILY OF MEMBERS OF YOUR GROUP

Usually you will meet someone at a networking or other meeting, and not know anything about their family. However, in many long term business turned friendship relationships (CAMARADERIE) you will meet members of that person's family. It could be their significant other, child or parent. Sometimes it is the family member who can benefit from something you can do to refer or introduce. If you can't help the networking friend, then perhaps you can help one of their family members.

STORY - TRAVEL AGENT

I met Rob several years ago at a networking meeting. His business was in international trade negotiations, and I could tell early on that it was probably unlikely that I could make a direct referral to him. He referred me for a move, and hired me to do a residential move for him. I liked Rob and wanted to reciprocate in some way. I met his wife, who is a travel agent, and happened to be planning a European trip. I talked to his wife and ended up hiring her to plan a trip for me. So even though I could not make a referral or introduction to Rob, I was able to reciprocate by hiring his wife. There are times when you have to be creative and find alternative ways of being of service to others.

TIP #82 - THE DEGREE OF KNOW, LIKE AND TRUST WILL DETERMINE FREQUENCY AND ENTHUSIASM OF REFERRALS AND INTRODUCTIONS

Know, Like and Trust are keys to the referral and introduction process. Additionally, it is really the degree/level of each component that drives the referral process. So if you know someone and what they do really well, like and trust them to a high degree, you are more likely to make a referral or introduction. As relationships develop, it is hopeful that you can engender a high level of KNOW, LIKE and TRUST with people you meet. Referrals should be based on the genuine belief that business could be transacted. They should never be bogus or gratuitous.

TIP #83 - DON'T MAKE FINAL JUDGMENTS BASED ON APPEARANCE

Appearance does matter, in some cases VERY MUCH. People often do judge on our appearance and attire. However, don't make final judgments based totally on a person's appearance and attire. There could be extenuating circumstances that lead them to dress in a particular way or for a particular occasion. If a person's appearance is unusual at one event, try to be open minded about the meaning of that appearance. A great example is Halloween.

TIP #84- ALWAYS BE ETHICAL AND HONEST

Ethics is an integral aspect of networking. ALWAYS be honest and ethical in your business practices. By conducting your business in an ethical manner, others will build and maintain trust in you. Don't sell people things they don't need. Honor your commitments. Admit it when you make a mistake or miss a meeting or deadline. There is no substitute for honesty and ethics.

TIP #85 - PACE YOURSELF IN NETWORKING EVENTS

There is a genuine danger of burnout in networking. I have experienced it myself and heard stories from others about taking a break from networking because of simply getting tired of it. It can be very intense, especially if you are actively building relationships (which you should be doing). I suggest pacing yourself and being consistent in your attendance of networking events, rather than trying to do a lot at one time. It is preferable to attend fewer events and to be consistent over a long period of time rather than bunching it into a compressed period and then taking a break. Vary the types of events from educational meetings, regular meeting and mixers.

TIP #86 - USE HUMOR, BUT BE AWARE OF SENSITIVE TOPICS

Humor can be a GREAT way to connect with others. In fact, humor has the potential to connect you in ways that only funny stuff can do. I have noticed that the one thread that I have with very close friends is humor, mentioning or discussing things that we find particularly funny. Each relationship is a bit different, and you will know when you have struck a common chord. There are limits to humor, and you have to be careful not to offend others. What one person finds funny another might find highly offensive. Use common sense to determine when and where to explore your use of humor, especially material on the raunchy side.

STORY- FUNNY MAN

In my long networking career, I have met MANY financial advisors, financial planners, investment advisors and others in the field of financial management. There are a lot of them in the networking world. I was at a troika with a man named Barry, and candidly told him that though he might be very good at what he did, it was unlikely that I would be able to refer him because I already knew so many people who did similar things. But he was VERY funny and did spot on impressions. He had me laughing heartily at his impressions. I spoke to a networking group that night, and told the story of Barry as an illustration of the referral process. A woman raised her hand after I was raving about his humor, and asked if I could refer her to Barry. So by his unique talent Barry had leapt over many existing financial professionals to get a referral. You never know when you might do or say something that differentiates you in a memorable and beneficial way.

TIP #87 - THERE IS NO SUBSTITUTE FOR COMPETENCE

All networking is based on COMPETENCE. You must do the best possible job in order to be worthy of referrals and strategic introductions. The TRUST component of the networking paradigm rests squarely on your level of competence. Always do the best possible job by being reliable, fair, thorough and performing high quality work. Without this component, your networking efforts will be wasted.

TIP #88 - DON'T BURN BRIDGES

There are times when we have a bad experience with another person, and times when we get angry. Despite that, resist the temptation to "burn bridges" and write someone permanently out of your business life. People and situations change, and it is preferable to keep your options open and remain open to others, even those who you have had a bad experience with in business. You never know when people might circle back into your life or how you or they might have changed or grown.

TIP #89 - UNDER PROMISE AND OVER DELIVER

When you say you are going to do something, it is wise to make sure that you can complete it in the time that you promise. It is much better to under promise and complete the task before you say you are going to complete it, rather than being overly optimistic and having to go back to the person and ask for an extension in time. Though it is tempting to promise something quicker, that is not usually best. For example, in setting appointments, allow for traffic and unforeseen circumstances, and suggest a window of time if possible rather than a firm time.

TIP #90 - BE GENUINE

In all cases it important to be genuine, and never to be phony. People respond much better to others who are real and sincere in their demeanor. One of the main reasons that people are likable is that they are genuine. Networking is NOT about putting on a fake smile and saying things you don't mean. It is much better to be real than to act like you know or like someone when you really don't. Don't be afraid to be vulnerable is the situation warrants it. Honesty is the best policy.

TIP #91 - THERE SHOULD BE A BALANCE BETWEEN TALKING AND LISTENING

Every conversation is different, and people differ in how much they typically speak and listen. In general, there should be a balance in how much you talk and how much you listen. To be an effective networker, you need to be good at both. Always be a good listener, and be prepared to talk when someone says, "What about you" or "Tell me about yourself" or "Tell me about your work." In sum, be interested and be interesting. High levels of both will lead to fruitful relationships. If there is an imbalance, work on your listening and speaking skills, because you cannot control others, and you can control yourself. Maintain a level of curiosity about people.

TIP #92 - ARRIVE EARLY AND STAY LATE

In order to get the most of networking meetings and social events, it is best to arrive early and to stay late. That is ideal and not always possible. Arriving early allows you to get comfortable, greet everyone as they arrive, and have an advantage in terms of social interaction over people who arrive late. You simply have more time to connect with others. Staying late offers similar benefits.

Full Disclosure - Personally, I do tend to arrive early and leave right after a meeting. I am working on the stay late component, as I know it is preferable.

TIP #93 - RESPECT PEOPLE'S TIME

Be aware that many people are quite busy, and their time is valuable. In different times, salespeople and others would take a long period of time to make their presentations. Today, especially in large urban areas, business people are not inclined to take as much time for such presentations. If you are urged to elaborate more fully on a point, do so. But don't drone on especially when you are getting verbal or nonverbal signs to "wrap it up."

TIP #94- HAVE GOOD BOUNDARIES WITHOUT BEING RIGID

It is important that you have good boundaries in terms of what you are willing to talk about and when you are open to talk. If someone asks questions that you feel are private, just respond directly that you would rather not talk about a particular topic. In so doing, don't be rigid, just firm. There are times when your original intention is NOT to talk about certain things, but situations lead you to modify your boundary.

TIP #95 - BE WARM

People respond more to people who are warm and welcoming. Perhaps this is not really teachable, but don't hesitate to show warmth to others in a business setting. If you are cold and aloof, people will not build as strong of relationships with you. This can take the form of hugging when you know a person better.

TIP #96 - DON'T EXAGGERATE

When telling stories and describing events, there is a a tendency to exaggerate to make the story better. Though tempting, it is unwise to stretch the truth. Stick with the facts, and there will be plenty of times when reality is interesting enough.

TIP #97 - THE SIZE AND SCOPE OF YOUR NETWORK IS A PERSONAL CHOICE

It is really up to you to decide how large you want your network to be. You can keep it small and have very strong ties with everyone in it, or can widen it to include people who aren't particularly close to you. Social media allows you to make your network as wide as you want. It is okay to go quite wide and then deepen the network later or reduce who you contact.

TIP #98 - IT IS OKAY AND NATURAL TO HANG OUT WITH PEOPLE YOU ALREADY KNOW

When you have been in networking groups for awhile, you will naturally build relationships with some people that are deeper than others. People become friends, and it is only natural that you look forward to seeing and hanging out with them at events. Though you should be polite to people you don't know, it is perfectly fine to spend more time deepening existing relationships. When you are newer to networking and want to meet a lot of people, then it is probably better to mingle and forge new relationships.

TIP #99 - BE ENTHUSIASTIC IN YOUR INTERACTIONS WITH OTHERS, ESPECIALLY PEOPLE YOU REALLY LIKE

When you connect with people and find people you really like a lot, be enthusiastic in your interactions with them. It is fine to be professional and a bit reserved in the early stages of relationships. But when you find a kindred spirit, be willing to express a high level of excitement when you see them.

TIP #100 - SELF-AWARENESS IS KEY TO NETWORKING SUCCESS

To be fully successful in networking, it is vital to be aware of yourself and what impact you have on others. Know your strengths. If you are especially likable, detail oriented, patient, driven, fair or whatever aspect of your personality leads to your success, you should know it and capitalize on it. Some people are great at hard work, others at getting along with others. Whatever your positive characteristics are, be aware of them.

TIP #101 - DON'T ANSWER THE PHONE IF YOU DON'T WANT TO TALK

If you are busy or simply don't want to talk at a particular time, then don't pick up the phone. I realize there might be a temptation to reflexively answer the phone despite your situation, but resist that tendency. People will likely leave a message and you can call them when you are ready to fully engage them.

TIP #102 - BE AWARE OF TENDENCIES TOWARD PERFECTIONISM AND COMPLETION

Everyone has a tendency to be more perfectionistic or more oriented toward the punctual completion of tasks. Be aware of where you fall on this continuum, and be tolerant of others who have a different orientation than you. Neither tendency is the correct way, and you might focus differently depending on the importance or particular nature of the situation.

TIP #103 - NETWORKING IS NOT SELLING

Networking is not the same as selling. In fact, the less you directly or aggressively sell, the more effective you will be in networking. Focus on building mutually beneficial and productive relationships. Selling should take place separately from networking, or after you have a referral and are working with a potential customer or client.

NETWORKING EXERCISES

The following networking exercises have been used effectively in various networking groups. The leader/facilitator needs to consider time factors, the level of familiarity that the group members have with one another, and the purpose of the exercise. In all cases, the exercise should be fully explained in advance of starting. For some exercises, it is more important to allow people time to prepare rather than springing it on them at the meeting. As a leader, it is probably best to only do one exercise per meeting and really focus on it. It should be noted and emphasized that these exercises are only as good as the group leader or facilitator who leads them. Factors such as allotted time, group size, diversity within the group, room configuration, group dynamics, purpose and other things can have a major influence on the exact process and ultimate success of the exercises. Some of them require preparation by the participants, and others can be done more on the spur of the moment. There is much skill involved in facilitating these exercises, but it is most important to remain positive, patient and nurturing. Take the opportunity to use the blank spaces on these pages to make notes as you plan to use these exercises in your groups.

EXERCISE #1 - SHARING SOMETHING UNIQUE OR UNUSUAL ABOUT YOURSELF

In this exercise, the leader simply starts and says "Please share something that is unique, unusual or surprising about yourself." The leader could start by giving an example like "I have run 6 marathon races." The goal of this exercise is to share something that is memorable and not business related. A variation of this exercise is to first break people up into dyads (groups of two) and share the unique thing, then bring it back to the larger group.

EXERCISE #2 - WHAT IS THE BEST ADVICE YOU EVER RECEIVED AND DID YOU FOLLOW IT?

This exercise is designed to learn about the motivational factors that might have influenced someone. It also can tap into role models and the reasons that people behave in certain ways.

EXERCISE #3 - WHAT NICKNAMES HAVE YOU BEEN CALLED IN YOUR LIFE?

This is a fun exercise, that always brings some laughter and can lead to some follow up monikers. The leader might warn people that if they share a nickname, some people might start calling them by that name permanently.

EXERCISE #4 - WHAT SKILL OR HOBBY DO YOU MOST ENJOY OUTSIDE OF WORK?

This exercise allows others a glimpse into the "back of your business card" and gives people the chance to share a skill like playing the guitar, gourmet cooking, gardening or word games. It also focusses on the personal side, which can really enhance the blossoming of relationships. Additionally, it can lead to social encounters like going to theater, playing golf or going on hikes together.

EXERCISE #5 - SOLVING A PROBLEM BY BRINGING IN OUR COLLECTIVE SKILLS

In this exercise, the leader starts by proposing a scenario that requires various professional skills to solve a problem. For example, the leader could state, "Bob and Sue are a married couple who are going through a divorce. Their children are nearing college age, they don't have a living trust, and Sue wants to go to grad school." Then the members of the group can state how they could hypothetically assist this family. There could be a family law attorney, college counselor, wills and estates specialist, psychotherapist and financial advisor. This is a fun exercise that can provide both real and humorous approaches to the problem. To enhance its effectiveness, encourage people to make up pieces of the situation if it doesn't lend itself to a genuine contribution. Have fun with it and the participants will learn and remember more.

EXERCISE #6 - LIKABILITY DISCUSSION

In this exercise, you break the group into pairs (dyads). It is important that it is only groups of two people. They are then instructed to talk about a topic (exact topic not important). After they have had about 5-10 minutes, you then go back to the big group. The question the leader asks is "What was likable about the person you were paired with?" It is not necessary that every dyad gives feedback, and the instructions emphasize that only positive characteristics are mentioned.

EXERCISE #7 - ELEVATOR SPEECH PRACTICE: LESS IS MORE

This exercise allows participants to work on their elevator speeches by reducing the number of words they use to describe what they do. The goal is one word, but that is not always possible. For example, for my relocation business I could simply say Moves. In my consulting training, I could say Networking, but Networking Coach is better. So some times you will have to use more than one word, but if it is appropriate for your profession or brand, less is more.

EXERCISE #8 - PERCEPTION CHECK

This exercise considers the differences between self-perception and the various perception of others. Each person will start with one characteristic that they would use to describe themselves, and then others will comment on their perception. In running this exercise, it is important to stress remaining positive. Though negative characteristics might come up, they are not the main focus. For example, someone might describe themselves as shy, and another might perceive them as withdrawn. This exercise takes some real skill on the part of the facilitator or group leader.

EXERCISE #9 - FREEING OR BINDING RESPONSES

This activity involves a two-way communication in which questions are asked by one person.

It is meant to differentiate between open-ended questions (freeing) like "Tell me about your business" and closed-ended (binding) questions like "Do you like your work" which only require one word answers. The goal is to teach members about the benefit of asking more freeing questions.

EXERCISE #10 - REMEMBERING NAMES

This is a great exercise designed to learn and remember names, and it is fun. It really works well in groups under 15. Here is how it works. Everyone is asked to think of an appropriate (or fun) adjective to put before their first name that begins with the same letter as the person's name. For example, I might be Baseball Bill. As you go around the room (and you have to go in order), each succeeding person repeats the names (with monikers) of everyone who precedes them. So it is really the repetition that locks in the memory. The group leader should jump in and assist those who might be struggling.

EXERCISE #11 - INTRODUCING OTHERS

This is a great exercise for any networking group, new or forming. You break people into groups of two. Allow about 5 minutes for the discussion between the two people. Each person is to take about 2 1/2 minutes to describe their work/profession. The listener can take notes if they want. After both people have had the opportunity to speak, everyone returns to the big group. Then each person introduces the other person, and more and more accurately they describe the other person the better.

EXERCISE #12 - STRENGTH BOMBARDMENT

This exercise works very well in seasoned groups, where a positive rapport and group dynamic is in place. People should also know a bit about others. It is done on a volunteer basis. A person will volunteer, and the others are encouraged to share positive things about the volunteer, such as: You are a great worker, you are a team player, you are inspirational. So you are bombarding people with your perception of their strengths and positive characteristics.

EXERCISE #13 - BACK OF THE BUSINESS CARD

This exercise allows participants to share something about themselves that is not at all related to business. People are asked to share something about the "back of the business card". This activity leads to deepening of relationships and highlights the personal rather than the business side of ourselves.

EXERCISE #14 - TWO TRUTHS AND A LIE

In this fun exercise each member (prepared in advance) brings three statements about themselves to the meeting and states them. Two of them are true,the third is untrue. The group then guesses which statement is untrue. The activity really opens people's eyes about others and exposes them to something about others. Another version or option is to make it EITHER two truths and a lie or three truths. In this variation/option the people make three statements, all of which are true.

EXERCISE #15 - GOLD MINE REFERRAL

This exercise allows participants to share a "gold mine"/career making referral. The question that the group leader asks is "What would be the best possible referral for you, something that would really jump start or even make your career?" This allows others to consider who they could possibly refer or introduce to that person.

EXERCISE #16 - VALUABLE SKILLS CHARACTERISTICS

The question to begin this exercise is "What specific skills or characteristics make you particularly valuable to your clients?" The answers allow others to really glimpse into the "value add" that members provide to their clients. It could be things like reliability, attention to detail, sensitivity, knowledge of their profession or fairness.

EXERCISE #17 - SECONDARY SKILLS/SPECIALTIES

This exercise allows participants to share a secondary skill or specialization that others might not know about. For example, if someone is a family law attorney and also a mediator, they can share the mediation skill while mentioning that they are also a family law attorney. This activity is best utilized with mature groups who are fully aware of people's main speciality.

EXERCISE #18 - SHARING VALUABLE TIP

In this exercise each participant is told in advance to plan to share a valuable tip about their business that could be useful to others. This allows everyone to demonstrate their expertise and experience. It is best used with more mature groups who already know the basics about fellow members. This can markedly increase trust among members.

EXERCISE #19 - THE EXTRA HOUR

What would you do if you had an extra hour each week? In this busy world, many people are time crunched and overwhelmed. They are asked in advance to discuss at the meeting what they would do if they had just one more hour each week. Most likely they will mention something like spending more time with family, enjoying a hobby or exercise.

EXERCISE #20 - WHAT WOULD YOU LIKE TO LEARN

In this activity members express something they would like to learn that they don't already know. Examples can be to play a musical instrument, surf, sail or cook.

EXERCISE #21 - WHERE WOULD YOU GO?

Each participant is asked to consider any place in the world that they would like to go to, if money was no barrier. They are instructed to describe the place, and why they chose it.

EXERCISE #22 - MOST CHALLENGING SITUATION IN YOUR LIFE

In this activity, people are asked to consider the most challenging, scary or precarious situation that they have ever been in, and to describe how they got out of it safely.

EXERCISE #23 - DISCUSSION ON LOYALTY IN REFERRALS

This discussion is designed more for experienced networkers. Consider loyalty and how many people you might refer to and when. Should you be loyal to one person, or can you successfully build a wide network and spread your referrals around to several or many people?

EXERCISE #24 - USING A PROP TO DESCRIBE YOUR WORK

In this exercise, participants are told well in advance of the meeting to bring a prop to the next meeting that describes in some way what they do. The more accurate to real profession is the goal. A brief story is recommended to accompany the prop if you have the time.

EXERCISE #25 - TEAM BUILDING CONTEST: STATE CAPITALS

The group is first divided into teams of five people each. No smart phones are allowed. Each group is given 10-15 minutes to come up with as many correct state capitals as possible. At the end of the allotted time, each team tallies up the number of state capitals. Than the group leader asks for the answers, and checks them against the correct state capitals.

EXERCISE #26 - WHAT IS FIRST THING YOU USUALLY NOTICE ABOUT ANOTHER PERSON

This exercise is designed to increase self-awareness and the awareness of others' perceptions. Participants are asked to consider the first thing they usually notice about others. Some possibilities are the following: hair, height, weight, clothes and age.

EXERCISE #27 - TALK ABOUT THE TURNING POINT IN YOUR LIFE

In this exercise, participants are instructed to talk about the defining event or situation that they believe to be the turning point in their life and/or career. They have the option to make it more personal or business focused.

EXERCISE #28 - SHARING A PICTURE FROM YOUR PERSONAL LIFE HIGHLIGHT FILM

This exercise requires group members to send in a photo of themselves prior to the meeting. The picture should represent some significant event from their life, such as when they finished a marathon, held their child, were on a dream vacation, or at some other key moment in their life (the more positive the better).

Then during the meeting, each picture would be projected and the person will briefly discuss the event or situation and the special meaning it holds for them.

EXERCISE #29 - FINDING THINGS IN COMMON

In this exercise, first the group leader breaks up the large group into groups of 4-5 people. Once the smaller groups are formed, they are instructed to make a list of things they have in common (other than being human beings and members of the group/organization). The starting point is usually suggestions like travel to Europe, riding a bicycle, liking a certain food or drink, or having a skill or hobby. The goal is to find as many commonalities as possible within a 5-10 minute time span.

EXERCISE #30 - WHEN WERE YOU REALLY SURPRISED?

This exercise allows participants to tell a story about a time in thier life when they were especially surprised by what another person told them or did. It can be a time when someone revealed something about themselves that took them aback, and how this revelation changed their thinking and/or assumptions about the other person. This exercise is best done in dyads (two people), who then bring the revelation back to the larger group.

EXERCISE #31 - SHARING POSITIVE PERCEPTIONS

In this activity, participants are asked to share a perception of another person (ONLY POSITIVE ONES) such as "I feel very comfortable around you" or "I really trust your judgment". The goal is to raise awareness and help people see how other people perceive them. If there is time, people can share more than one thing.

EXERCISE #32 - SHARING EXAMPLES OF LEARNING ABOUT A "SITUATION"

Sometimes we have a negative perception of another person, but come to realize that something unusual, unpleasant or stressful was happening in their life like a medical condition, grief or change in relationship status was a primary reason. Participants are asked to share an actual situation when they had one impression of someone, but learned to cut them some slack when they learned about something that was causing someone to behave in a negative or unpleasant way.

EXERCISE #33 - WHAT'S ON YOUR DESK?

This exercise asks participants to share a few items that are "on their desk" to provide a flavor of their actual work. Each person shares some things that are currently on their desk and requiring their attention. Others can then ask for elaboration or clarification.

EXERCISE #34 - AGE PREFERENCE

In this exercise, participants are asked to share whether they prefer to socialize with others who are younger than them, older than them, or roughly the same age. They are also asked to share their reasons for these preferences. The purpose of this exercise is to determine some of the meanings of these preferences.

EXERCISE #35 - SHARING A FUNNY EXPERIENCE OR SITUATION

This exercise should definitely be done by giving participants some time to think about it in advance. They are asked to share something that happened to them that was extremely funny. It could be a situation, an event or anything that really made them laugh and continues to amuse them when they recall it.

SOME TIPS ON LEADING A NETWORKING GROUP

Though this is primarily a book about how to be an effective networker and to make meaningful and beneficial relationships, there are some skills related to leading networking groups. The better the group leader, the more likely there will be commerce, camaraderie and community that is fostered therein. Group leaders need to set the proper tone, and be welcoming to people who are part of their group as well as guests to the group. Many of the skills mentioned in the Tip section of the book apply also to group leaders.

A basic starting point is the use of TIME. As a leader you must be aware of time and never give the group members the feeling of being rushed. I recommend that you cover the important business earlier in the meeting so that you don't run out of time or feel undue pressure to complete your primary business. Let people know how much time they have to make their elevator speeches and any other topic, and be willing to politely cut them off if they are going over their limit. Another viable option is to appoint a timekeeper to let people know when their time is up. Own the room! You are in charge, and you need to run the meeting and not let the meeting run you. You can do this with grace without seeming to be too bossy or autocratic.

Learn people's names and call them by name. It is not necessary, or even advisable to simply go around the room for introductions or when discussing topics. If you really focus on who has spoken, you can call on people until everyone has had the opportunity to speak. By skipping around people are more likely to stay alert because they never know when you are going to call on them. Stay positive and create a positive tone in your group. Negativity is not useful in promoting a proper atmosphere and climate.

Show up well in advance of the starting time, so that you can be sure that the room is set up properly, and so you can greet people when they arrive. Be a warm and welcoming host. You set the tone from the minute the doors open. Get a sense when the "critical mass" of attendees are present, and then call the meeting to order.

Either do that in a forceful yet polite manner, or ask someone else to be the "muscle."

As the leader you should be a good role model in terms of being prepared, showing up consistently and treating everyone with kindness. It all starts and ends with you, and the better job you do, the better atmosphere will be created for the cultivation of camaraderie, commerce and a genuine sense of community with your group and the larger organization.

As a group leader, you need to develop skills in both running a meeting and running a group. The skills are different but equally important. If you are aware of a weakness in either, build an executive committee to assist you in the areas where you need help. Meet with your EC on a regular basis to build rapport and strong working relationships. It is useful (and fun) to share a meal with the executive committee and to show gratitude frequently and enthusiastically.

Don't rush people. Create a relaxed atmosphere where people feel comfortable to speak and be heard.

Don't deny your own personality or try to be just like someone else who is a successful group leader. Above all, BE YOURSELF. Every group really is different, and there is no one right way to facilitate a group.

SOURCES FOR NETWORKING TIPS, STORIES, AND EXERCISES

So where did all of this material come from? There are several major sources and many less influential ones. The number one source is Bruin Professionals, a UCLA alumni association. I am currently Executive Vice President (President Elect) for Bruin Professionals. The other highly influential group is ProVisors, where I am a Group Leader of a chapter in Downtown Los Angeles, have been a trainer and have spoken widely on networking skills.

The material in the book is also influenced by prior membership in chambers of commerces, trade organizations, service clubs, alumni groups, civic organizations, regional and national conferences and the training of professional firms.

I have spoken on all aspects of the psychological and practical aspects of networking such as law firms, accounting firms, real estate firms, universities, networking groups, and other professional groups throughout the United States. I also write a blog on my web site drbillsaleebey.com.

CONCLUSION

This is a book about professional networking, and the intention of the author is to impart any and every important networking skill possible. Though the main focus is to build business and promote commerce among networkers, it is also about networking as a way of an ethical life. The bias is clearly about being a GIVER, and through an attitude of trying to help others everyone will benefit and we will build meaningful and mutually beneficial relationships over time.

The approach of this type of networking assumes that there are significant differences among people in various regions, of various ages and cultures, and in widely differing types of work. There is not one RIGHT way to network in all situations. Some times it is highly preferable to listen, and in others you need to be able to talk. The assumption here is that there is an inherent value of networking, and that everyone has a different level to which they want to build and nurture their network. But if you want to build a vibrant and nourishing network, this book told you how to do it. If you are really diligent and actively practice all of the networking tips, you will be guaranteed success. Even if you only practice most of them your life will be better because of it.

In some situations you will be limited about the possible groups or organizations you can join. In other cases the possibilities are virtually limitless. It is beyond the purview of this book to offer specific advice on how many groups or even how much time that you spend networking. The main things to remember are to treat everyone with respect, be a good listener, try to help others in any way you can, stay in touch with others and do the best job you can possibly do.

BIBLIOGRAPHY

Acuff, Jerry. The Relationship Edge. Hoboken, NJ: John Wiley and Sons, Inc., 2007.

Asher, Joey. Selling and Communication Skills for Lawyers. New York: ALM Publishing, 2005.

Bjorseth, Lillian D. Breakthrough Networking: Building Relationships that Last. Lisle, IL: Duoforce Press, 2003.

Burg, Bob. Endless Referrals. New York: McGraw-Hill, 2005.

Burg, Bob & John David Mann. The Go Giver. Deckle Edge Publishing, 2007.

De Santis, James. The Business of Practice. Glendale: De Santis Publications, 2011.

Ferrazzi, Keith. Never Eat Alone. New York: Doubleday Press, 2005.

Fisher, Donna and Sandy Vilas. Power Networking. Austin: Bard Press, 2000.

Fraser, George C. Click. New York: McGraw-Hill, 2008.

Gitomer, Jeffrey. Little Black Book of Connections. Austin: Bard Press, 2006.

Grant, Adam. Give and Take. New York: Penguin Publishing, 2013.

Mackay, Harvey. Dig Your Well Before You're Thirsty. New York: Doubleday, 1990.

Nierenberg, Andrea. Nonstop Networking: How to Improve Your Life, Luck and Career. Sterling, VA: Capital Books, 2002.

Saleebey, Dennis. The Strengths Perspective in Social Work (5th Ed.). Boston: Allyn & Bacon, 2006.

Saleebey, William M. Connecting: Beyond the Name Tag.   Los Angeles: Believe Publishing, 2009.

Saleebey, William M. Sell Yourself. Santa Monica: Mentor Publishing, 1994.

Salmon, Michael. Super Networking. Franklin Lakes: Career Press, 2004.

Savar, Sheila. The Power of Networking. Reston, VA: Bama Press, 2008.

Templeton, Tim. The Referral of a Lifetime. San Francisco: Berrett-Koehler Publishers, 2005.

Warner, Jon. Networking Pocketbook. Aurlesford: Laurel House, 2008.

Zack, Devora. Networking for People who Hate Networking. San Francisco: Berrett-Koehler Publishers, 2010.